All About Mom
Memory Journal

(I didn't know that about you!)
Prompted Journal for Mom

Megan Adams

To Mom...I always knew you were an amazing Mom. Thank you for giving me the chance to get to know what a wonderful and interesting woman you are.

Journals available by Megan Adams
I didn't know that about you!
Series of Prompted Journals

All About Mom Memory Journal
Prompted Journal for Mom

All About Dad Memory Journal
Prompted Journal for Dad

All About Grandma Memory Journal
Prompted Journal for Grandma

All About Grandpa Memory Journal
Prompted Journal for Grandpa

All About Mom Memory Journal
(I didn't know that about you!)
Prompted Journal for Mom

First Printing, 2017
ISBN 978-1542650618

Use this journal to capture the memories that make you so special to your family. The journal is divided into sections with empty pages at the end of each if you wish to tell extra stories or include other information. Fill out as much or as little as you want. Change the questions to fit your life and add topics that are specific to you. I hope that this journal brings back special times and thoughts for you. Your family will always treasure your memories. Enjoy.

Table of Contents

Childhood Memories

Family life — 2
Food and Meals — 10
School — 12
Under the weather — 16
Grandparents — 18
Holidays — 20
Fun — 24

Adult Memories

Work — 32
Travel — 34
Adventure — 36
Love — 38

Parenting

Babies — 46
Children — 48

The World Around You

Fashion — 58
Food — 60
Events — 62
Technology — 64

About You

Beliefs — 74
Thoughts — 76
Advice — 82

Childhood
Memories

Who did you live with as a child? (list relatives full names...for siblings note how much older and/or younger each was):

_____

_____

_____

_____

_____

_____

_____

_____

_____

_____

_____

_____

When and where were you born?

_____

_____

_____

_____

_____

What did your Mom and Dad do for a living?

_____

_____

_____

_____

_____

_____

_____

_____

What was your bedroom like? Did you share it? Decorate it?

_____

_____

_____

_____

_____

_____

_____

_____

What kind of chores did you have?

_____

_____

_____

_____

_____

Did you get along with your brothers/sisters? Was there a favorite?

_____

_____

_____

_____

_____

What kind of vehicle did your family own? Where did you sit?

_____

_____

_____

_____

_____

Did you consider your family poor, average, rich?

_____

_____

_____

_____

_____

Were your parents strict? What did you get for a punishment?

_____

_____

_____

_____

_____

Did you have any pets?

_____

_____

_____

_____

What was the best and worst trait about your Mother?

_____

_____

_____

_____

_____

_____

_____

_____

What was the best and worst trait about your Father?

_____

_____

_____

_____

_____

_____

_____

_____

What was the best thing about having siblings? (if you didn't have any, what was best about being an only child?)

_____

_____

_____

_____

_____

_____

_____

_____

What was the worst thing about having siblings? (if you didn't have any, what was worst about being an only child?)

_____

_____

_____

_____

_____

_____

_____

_____

Where did you live as a child? If you moved what was it like to move to a new place?

_____

_____

_____

_____

_____

_____

_____

_____

_____

_____

_____

_____

_____

_____

_____

_____

_____

_____

_____

_____

_____

What kind of vacations did your family go on?

_____

_____

_____

_____

_____

_____

_____

_____

What was your best family vacation?

_____

_____

_____

_____

_____

_____

_____

_____

List 3 of your favorite home cooked meals...

_____

_____

_____

_____

_____

What was your favorite dessert?

_____

_____

_____

_____

_____

What meal or food was a special treat?

_____

_____

_____

_____

Food and Meals

How often did you go out to eat? Did your family have a
favorite?

_____

_____

_____

_____

_____

Did you do any cooking or baking?

_____

_____

_____

_____

_____

What food or meal did you hate as a kid?

_____

_____

_____

_____

_____

Did you like school?   Was it hard or easy for you?

_____

_____

_____

_____

_____

What kind of school did you attend?

_____

_____

_____

_____

_____

Did you walk or ride a bus? How far was it?

_____

_____

_____

_____

_____

What was your favorite subject? Why?

_____

_____

_____

_____

_____

_____

_____

_____

_____

What was your worst subject? Why?

_____

_____

_____

_____

_____

_____

_____

_____

_____

What was a typical school lunch like?

_____

_____

_____

_____

_____

_____

Were you in any clubs?

_____

_____

_____

_____

_____

_____

Did you play sports in school?

_____

_____

_____

_____

_____

School

Did you ever get in trouble at school?

_____

_____

_____

_____

_____

_____

How big was your high school?

_____

_____

_____

_____

_____

_____

What did you want to be when you grew up?

_____

_____

_____

_____

Did you get sick a lot when you were a kid?

_____

_____

_____

_____

_____

_____

Did you get the measles or mumps?

_____

_____

_____

_____

_____

_____

Did you break any bones?

_____

_____

_____

_____

_____

Do you have any scars?

_____

_____

_____

_____

_____

Did someone in your family get sick or injured?

_____

_____

_____

_____

_____

What was going to the dentist like?

_____

_____

_____

_____

Describe your Grandmother(s):

_____

_____

_____

_____

_____

Did (does) she have a special trait, recipe or tradition?

_____

_____

_____

_____

_____

Please share a special memory of her:

_____

_____

_____

_____

_____

Describe your Grandfather(s):

_____

_____

_____

_____

_____

_____

Did (does) he have a special trait, recipe or tradition?

_____

_____

_____

_____

_____

_____

Please share a special memory of him:

_____

_____

_____

_____

_____

Did you celebrate Halloween? How?

_____

_____

_____

_____

_____

Did the toothfairy visit you? Give you money?

_____

_____

_____

_____

_____

Did you get an Easter Basket?

_____

_____

_____

_____

What religion were you raised?

_____

_____

_____

_____

_____

Did you/How did you celebrate Christmas?

_____

_____

_____

_____

_____

Did you pray?

_____

_____

_____

_____

_____

What was your favorite holiday? Why?

_____

_____

_____

_____

_____

What was a family holiday tradition?

_____

_____

_____

_____

_____

Who did you celebrate important holidays with?

_____

_____

_____

_____

_____

How did your family celebrate your birthday? Do you remember any birthday as being extra special?

_____

_____

_____

_____

_____

What was your best birthday present?

_____

_____

_____

_____

_____

What was your favorite birthday cake?

_____

_____

_____

_____

_____

Who was your best friend(s)?

_____

_____

_____

_____

_____

What did you and your friends do for fun?

_____

_____

_____

_____

_____

Did you have sleepovers? A secret hideout?

_____

_____

_____

_____

Fun

What was your favorite toy?

_____

_____

_____

_____

_____

What indoor games did you play?

_____

_____

_____

_____

_____

What outdoor games did you play?

_____

_____

_____

_____

_____

Childhood Memories

Childhood Memories

Adult
Memories

What was your first full time job?

_____

_____

_____

_____

_____

If you could have had a different career what would it be?

_____

_____

_____

_____

_____

What types of Education/Training have you had?

_____

_____

_____

_____

Work

What was something you're proud of regarding work?

_____

_____

_____

_____

_____

What was your best job?

_____

_____

_____

_____

_____

What was your worst job?

_____

_____

_____

_____

_____

What are the two best places you have visited?

_____

_____

_____

_____

_____

Where do you wish you had gone, or would like to go?

_____

_____

_____

_____

_____

Do you wish you had traveled more? If yes, where?

_____

_____

_____

_____

What was the worst place you visited?

_____

_____

_____

_____

_____

_____

If you could have a second home anywhere, where would it be?

_____

_____

_____

_____

_____

Do you prefer exciting or relaxing vacations?

_____

_____

_____

_____

What are the two most daring, adventurous or dangerous things you've done?

What interesting activities have you tried?

_____

_____

_____

_____

_____

_____

_____

_____

_____

What are two unusual foods you've tried? Were they better or worse than you expected?

_____

_____

_____

_____

_____

_____

_____

_____

_____

Who was your first crush/love?

_____

_____

_____

_____

_____

How long were you and Dad together before you had children?

_____

_____

_____

_____

_____

What is the nicest or most romantic thing Dad ever did for you?

_____

_____

_____

_____

Love

What kind of wedding did you have?

_____

_____

_____

_____

_____

Where did you go for your honeymoon?

_____

_____

_____

_____

_____

What was/is the best part about marriage?

_____

_____

_____

_____

_____

Adult Memories

Adult Memories

Adult Memories

Parenting
Memories

Did you plan on how many kids you wanted?

_____

_____

_____

_____

_____

_____

What was pregnancy like?

_____

_____

_____

_____

_____

_____

What was childbirth like?

_____

_____

_____

_____

_____

_____

What did you feed your baby?

_____

_____

_____

_____

_____

_____

Who helped take care of your kid(s)?

_____

_____

_____

_____

_____

_____

Did you read to your child(ren)?

_____

_____

_____

_____

_____

Describe three scary events/injuries with your child(ren):

_____

_____

_____

_____

_____

_____

_____

_____

_____

_____

_____

_____

_____

_____

_____

_____

_____

_____

_____

_____

_____

_____

_____

What do you wish you had done more of with your children?

_____

_____

_____

_____

_____

_____

_____

_____

What do you wish you had done less of with your children?

_____

_____

_____

_____

_____

_____

_____

_____

Do you think you were strict, moderate or easy on your kid(s)?

_____

_____

_____

_____

_____

_____

Do you think you expected too much/just right/not enough of your child(ren)?

_____

_____

_____

_____

_____

_____

Were you overprotective?

_____

_____

_____

_____

_____

Children

What did you enjoy doing with your kids?

_____

_____

_____

_____

_____

What games did you play with your child(ren)?

_____

_____

_____

_____

_____

What was the hardest thing about raising kids?

_____

_____

_____

_____

_____

Parenting Memories

The World
Around You

Share a memory about the following fashions:

Bell bottoms or designer jeans

_____

_____

_____

_____

_____

Leg warmers or shoulder pads

_____

_____

_____

_____

_____

Hot Pants, mini skirts, or tie-dye

_____

_____

_____

_____

_____

Fashion

Platform shoes, trendy boots or clogs

_____

_____

_____

_____

_____

_____

Favorite fashion trend?

_____

_____

_____

_____

_____

_____

Least favorite fashion trend?

_____

_____

_____

_____

_____

Share a memory of the following....

Fondue, Velveeta or Cheez Wiz

_____

_____

_____

_____

_____

_____

Oleo, lard, margarine or butter

_____

_____

_____

_____

_____

_____

TV dinners, breakfast cereals

_____

_____

_____

_____

_____

Food

Candy cigarettes or penny candy

_____

_____

_____

_____

_____

_____

Glass Coke bottles or soda fountains

_____

_____

_____

_____

_____

_____

Cream puffs, baked Alaska or ice cream trucks

_____

_____

_____

_____

_____

How were you or your family affected by, or what memories do you have of...

Gas Shortage

_____

_____

_____

_____

_____

_____

Wars/World Conflicts

_____

_____

_____

_____

_____

_____

Natural Disasters

_____

_____

_____

_____

_____

_____

9/11

_____

_____

_____

_____

_____

_____

Cold War/Nuclear Fears

_____

_____

_____

_____

_____

_____

_____ (one that stands out in your memory)

_____

_____

_____

_____

_____

When did you get your first cell phone? What kind was it?

_____

_____

_____

_____

_____

_____

Describe your first car:

_____

_____

_____

_____

_____

_____

How did you listen to music growing up?

_____

_____

_____

_____

_____

How did you watch movies growing up?

_____

_____

_____

_____

_____

When did you get your first computer?

_____

_____

_____

_____

_____

How did you look up information in High School?

_____

_____

_____

_____

_____

What was your experience or memories for the following?

VHS, Betamax Tapes

_____

_____

_____

_____

_____

_____

TV Antennas, Remote Controls

_____

_____

_____

_____

_____

_____

Computer floppy disks (8 inch, 5.5 inch, 3.5 inch)

_____

_____

_____

_____

_____

Music cassette tapes, albums

_____

_____

_____

_____

_____

_____

Pagers, fax machines

_____

_____

_____

_____

_____

_____

Rotary phone, answering machine

_____

_____

_____

_____

_____

_____

The World Around You

About You

Do you believe in the following? Have you ever experienced anything related to these?

Miracles

_____

_____

_____

_____

_____

Karma

_____

_____

_____

_____

_____

Ghosts

_____

_____

_____

_____

_____

Beliefs

Aliens

_____

_____

_____

_____

_____

_____

Guardian Angels

_____

_____

_____

_____

_____

_____

Love at First Sight

_____

_____

_____

_____

_____

List 2 skills or talents that you are glad you have:

_____

_____

_____

_____

_____

If you could be any age again, what would it be?

_____

_____

_____

_____

_____

What three characteristics would you like people to think of you as?

_____

_____

_____

_____

_____

Have you had your picture in the newspaper?

_____

_____

_____

_____

_____

_____

Have you ever won anything or been awarded something?

_____

_____

_____

_____

_____

Have you met any famous people?

_____

_____

_____

_____

_____

What days or events in your life have had the most impact on you?

_____

_____

_____

_____

_____

_____

_____

_____

_____

_____

_____

_____

_____

_____

_____

What are three of the nicest things someone has done for you?

_____

_____

_____

_____

_____

_____

_____

_____

_____

_____

_____

_____

_____

_____

_____

What has been your biggest challenge?

_____

_____

_____

_____

_____

What have you disliked about growing older?

_____

_____

_____

_____

_____

What have you liked about growing older?

_____

_____

_____

_____

_____

What do you wish you had known when you were younger?

_____

_____

_____

_____

_____

_____

How were things harder growing up then they are today?

_____

_____

_____

_____

_____

_____

How were things easier growing up then they are today?

_____

_____

_____

_____

_____

What advice do you have about the following:

Friends

_____

_____

_____

_____

_____

Family

_____

_____

_____

_____

_____

Marriage/Love

_____

_____

_____

_____

_____

Advice

Raising Children

_____
_____
_____
_____
_____
_____

Career

_____
_____
_____
_____
_____
_____

Growing older

_____
_____
_____
_____
_____

About You

About You

Made in the USA
Columbia, SC
12 March 2018